D1444936

The San Francisco Earthquake and Fire

About the Book

On April 18, 1906, the city of San Francisco was beginning to awaken to the warm Pacific breezes and soft blue skies of a spring morning. A minute and one-half later, San Francisco was in ruins, leveled by an earthquake which rolled through the city without warning. Fires erupted instantaneously and raged uncontrollably for days, burning to the ground whatever had remained standing in the city and surrounding areas. Many people were killed; more than 300,000 were homeless. Helen Markley Miller here presents a fascinating account of the city and its people, and how some survived the calamitous earthquake to rebuild a city destroyed.

EXTRA The San Francisco Examiner EXTRA

SAN FRANCISCO, FRIDAY, APRIL 20, 1906.

300,000 ARE HOMELESS, HUNGRY AND HELPLESS

THE PRICE OF THE TRIBUNE IS FIVE CENTS

150 MEN, WOMEN AND CHILDREN BURNED TO DEATH

San Francisco, April 21.—It is
people were burned to death
graph and Russian Hill
was raging the people we
recovered. Two ba

EXTRA Oakland Tribune. EXTRA

VOL. LXV   OAKLAND, CALIFORNIA—THURSDAY EVENING APRIL 19, 1906.   NO. 50

CITIZENS ARE FORCED TO FIGHT FLAMES AT POINT OF REVOLVER

Three hundred thousand persons will be left homeless
San Francisco by tonight. Help is needed at once.

THE OAKLAND HERALD   LAST EDITION

4:30   THE OAKLAND HERALD THURSDAY EVENING APRIL 19, 1906.   PRICE FIVE CENTS

FOURTH YEAR VOL. VII, NO. 45.

RAGING FLAMES STILL SPREAD; ALL SAN FRANCISCO SEEMS DOOMED

Great City Is Laid Waste by one of Worst Conflagrations in the History of Country

Spectators Appalled by Scenes of Terror Now Being Enacted in the Metropolis of the West

The San Francisco Earthquake and Fire

by Helen Markley Miller

Illustrated by Albert Orbaan

G. P. Putnam's
Sons
New York

Editorial Consultant:

Edna B. Ziebold, San Diego County Department of Education

Library of Congress Catalog Card Number:
73-102797

PRINTED IN THE UNITED STATES OF
AMERICA
12 up

979. 4
M.1

$5.99
1/78

Contents

1
Seconds of Terror

It was five o'clock on Wednesday morning, April 18, 1906. Dawn light lay over the city of San Francisco. A spring breeze from the Pacific came gently through the Golden Gate to fan away the night fog. Across the bay, where the sun would soon rise above the eastern hills, the sky was soft blue.

Most of the city's 450,000 people still slept, although smoke rose here and there from the chimneys of early risers. The streets were silent and deserted, except for policemen walking the last of their night's beats or tired newsmen, who had finished work on morning papers and now waited for the first streetcars. Near the northeastern, bay end of Market, the main business street that cut diagonally through the city to the southwest, men were astir in the produce district. They were piling sacks of vegetables into their drays from the old brick warehouses.

At eight minutes after five the streetlights went off for the day. At twelve minutes after the hour, the dray horses whinnied in alarm.

A second later, the earthquake struck!

There came a deep rumble, as if a giant, caged underground, raged for freedom. The rumble swelled to a deafening roar.

The earth shuddered. A twisting, back-and-forth motion shook the city—"as a terrier shakes a rat," one author wrote later. Then came a sickening roll. The ground rose and fell as do waves at sea.

Like trees in a gale, tall towers and spires whipped back and forth. Electric lines sagged and snapped. All electricity went off in the city. Steel rails, bridges, and streetcar cables tangled as if made of twine. Glass fronts fell away from stores and hotels. Chimneys crashed down on streets and rooftops. Frame houses splintered. Walls crumbled, pinning helpless people beneath the wreckage of ruined homes.

The first shock lasted thirty seconds.

Then came a dreadful silence. Awake now all over the city, survivors took deep breaths of relief. The earthquake was over.

Ten seconds of quiet. Then a second temblor came, more violent than the first. The roar returned in fury. Again the earth shook beneath the tortured city.

South of Market Street lay an area of shabby homes, rooming houses, and hotels. They had been built on fill and loose dirt over what had once been marsh, and underneath them the very earth gave way. Buildings lurched drunkenly or crashed down to trap or kill people beneath the wreckage. In some places the ground sank five feet. Pavements bulged up in waves.

The northeastern part of the city, near the bay wharves, had also been built on fill. The front wall of a jail fell, freeing its prisoners. In the wholesale and produce districts, brick walls crumbled on screaming horses and the men who tried to rescue their animals. The chimneys of the California Hotel crashed through the roof of a firehouse next door, destroying the stairs.

Fire Chief Dennis Sullivan, who had living quarters on the

third story, was fatally injured when he plunged through the empty stairwell to the first floor. San Francisco was now without a fire chief for the dangerous days ahead.

Southwest on Market was the new $6,000,000 City Hall. The first shock had begun its destruction; the second one completed it. Built of shoddy mortar, its walls and great pillars shattered, leaving only a skeleton of steel girders. In less than a minute the earthquake destroyed what had taken twenty years to build.

Nearby, the walls of the City Emergency Hospital hurtled inward to bury nurses, patients, and doctors under a weight of timber and plaster.

The second shock lasted for twenty-five seconds.

The roar faded, the angry earth stopped its mad dance, and silence came again.

In a little more than one minute, the earthquake had spread ruin and death over a proud city.

With the first shock, everyone not pinned beneath rubble had dashed outdoors for safety from crashing walls and roofs. The streets were crowded with dazed people. Parents gathered their families into close huddles. Little children, who did not understand disaster, laughed to see so many people so oddly dressed. A man in a tuxedo jacket above long johns wore three hats, one on top of the other. There were women in nightgowns, men in nightshirts. An old lady clutched a birdcage in one hand and with the other tugged a flannel bathrobe about her fat self. Few had bothered to find shoes, and bare feet bled from the splintered glass of broken windows.

At the Palace Hotel on Market Street, Enrico Caruso, the famous tenor, had been sleeping. He had sung Don José the night before in the New York Metropolitan Opera's production of *Carmen*. He awoke to find the furniture in his room reeling and tumbling. He clutched his precious throat. An old San

9

Francisco story has it that he rushed to the window, threw it open, and sang a few bars of the opera. He had to see if fright had scared away his voice. Seizing his autographed photograph of President Theodore Roosevelt, Caruso scrambled over the jumbled furniture to the door. In the hall he found the orchestra director of the opera company. The singer threw his arms around the man.

"I want nothing more to do with this place!" Caruso sobbed. "We are doomed! Doomed!"

After his outburst he dashed back into his room, packed a suitcase, and made his way to the lobby. There he sat on his valise, a towel wrapped around his throat, and muttered threats against a city where such chaos was allowed.

Young John Barrymore, the actor, also slept in San Francisco that morning. He awoke to the crashing of china in a friend's apartment. Dressing calmly, he went out to see the sights.

Another cool one was young Arnold Genthe, a photographer. Grabbing a camera, he hurried into the streets. His pictures of the destruction became one of the best records of the disaster.

Mrs. Kane, the matron of the Detention Hospital in the basement of the City Hall, panicked when the building started to collapse. Seizing the arm of the policeman on duty, John McLean, she ran for the safety of the street. Once there, she remembered with horror that she had left six insane patients locked in their cells. She pulled McLean back into the ruins. Together they rescued the patients and walked them across the city to the Presidio, near the Golden Gate. Mrs. Kane was not young but she went to work at once in the hospital there. For fifty-four hours without rest, she helped care for those injured by the quake.

In the better residential districts on the hills north and west of Market, earthquake damage had been slight. There, houses built of sturdier materials rested on bedrock foundations. People living there returned to their homes to find only shattered windows, jammed doors, and broken china. Some even went back to bed to finish sleeping. After all, it had only been another earthquake, and San Francisco was used to such shocks.

To those in the areas hardest hit, this was not "just another earthquake." It was a calamity. Many homes were nothing but kindling wood. Others tilted so dangerously that they could not be entered. The screams of the injured rose into the quiet air as men dug frantically to release the trapped from splintered timbers and fallen walls. Those who were safe could only thank God that they were alive.

2
Path of Disaster

What is an earthquake? It is a short and rapid vibration of the surface of the earth. But what causes the movement?

Our earth is a huge ball of stony material. Once the whole ball was molten rock, but over the slow ages its outer shell cooled. It shrank and folded and cracked to give us our beautiful mountains, valleys, and canyons. Sometimes the cracks are small but extremely deep; such a break in the earth's surface is called a fault. As the cooling of the crust goes deeper, pressure on the rock beneath increases. When the strain becomes too great at any one point, something has to give. Large masses of rock shift suddenly. The earth relieves itself of the terrific stress that has been built up by seeking the weakest point in its crust—the ancient fault. The result is an earthquake.

There are many of these faults in our world, and there are many earthquakes—some destructive and some so slight as to be scarcely noticed. The San Andreas Fault, on which San Francisco lies, runs almost the length of California's coastal mountains.

On that April morning in 1906 the city on the bay was not the only one to suffer the fury of the earthquake. All along the coast from Point Arena, 100 miles north of San Francisco, to Monterey, over 100 miles to the south, the quake spread its destruction in a path 20 to 40 miles wide.

Somewhere in the Pacific the quake had its beginning. The steamer *Arago*, off Point Arena in 12 fathoms of water, felt such a blow that the captain thought his ship had run aground.

The quake entered California just north of Point Arena, at Alder Creek. Its bridge splintered as the ground opened and closed again. The land west of the fault shifted 16 feet to the north of the earth on the opposite side. Masonry on the cone of the lighthouse on the point crashed down.

Southward the quake raced, ripping through towns and villages, tearing buildings from foundations, felling giant redwoods, leveling hills, and leaving great fissures in the ground.

At old Fort Ross, built by the Russians as a trading post in 1812 and abandoned by them in 1841, the quake toppled the two steeples of the old Russian Orthodox Church.

The town of Santa Rosa is 20 miles east of the San Andreas Fault, but waves from the temblor reached out to bring disaster. The entire business district and part of the residential area were demolished. The City Hall and the County Courthouse fell. In the building that housed the *Press Democrat,* the morning paper had just been run off the presses. Newsboys waited for papers to deliver. Three of them died under the rubble; one was pulled alive from the ruins. Santa Rosa counted seventy-five deaths that day.

The shuddering of the earth caused freakish deeds as it moved southward. At Tomales Bay it picked up the Marshall Hotel from its foundations on a headland and set it down in the water with its vacationing guests terrified, but unhurt. Out in the bay a huge wave lifted a fisherman's boat high and then receded to leave the boat stranded on shore. The wave returned to sweep the boat again into the bay.

13

At Point Reyes the morning train was ready for its daily run to the ferry at Sausalito. The train toppled over on its side. And not a single pane of glass in the coaches was shattered.

Near Olema at the Skinner Dairy, ranch hands were just beginning the morning milking. Cows and milkers were flung to the barn floor. When the men scrambled up, they found a changed scene outside. In front of the farmhouse, a row of cypress trees had bordered the country road, and between trees and house had been a rose garden. Trees and rose garden had moved into position in front of the barn. Raspberry bushes that had grown to the north of the house now filled the spot where the rose garden had been.

The earthquake moved out to sea north of San Francisco and then came swooping back to hit the city with all its force. Out in San Francisco Bay, the grim prison of Alcatraz stood unharmed, but waves of the temblor reached to the east side of the bay and struck the towns of Oakland and Berkeley. Damage there was not great, however.

South along the fault the quake rolled, shivering a dozen towns. It struck Palo Alto, to damage almost every building in the business district. In the town itself no human life was lost, however.

On the outskirts of Palo Alto was the fifteen-year-old Stanford University, the gift of millionaire Leland Stanford, one of the four men who had built the western half of the first transcontinental railway. Leland Stanford had spent generously to erect a fine university in memory of his son, who had died of a fever when he was fifteen years old.

When the earthquake had passed, most of the sandstone buildings on the campus lay in ruins. The library and the new gymnasium were wrecked. Encino Hall, the freshman dormitory, trapped many students in its fall and killed one. The beautiful mosaic front of the chapel collapsed outward when the clock

14

tower smashed through the roof. In arches built into the second story of the Science Building stood statues of famous scientists. The one of Louis Agassiz, Swiss-American geologist and zoologist, tumbled from its perch to bury head and shoulders in the pavement below.

"The head-foremost scientist in the United States," joked one student later.

A few miles to the south, the city of San Jose took the full brunt of the quake in ruined business buildings, churches, and homes. On the outskirts of the town was Agnew's State Hospital for the Insane. More than a thousand inmates were housed in its brick buildings. Walls and roofs crashed down on patients and nurses, killing more than a hundred.

"I'm going to heaven in a chariot of fire!" one patient screamed.

"Jesus of Nazareth is passing!" another shouted over and over.

A huge madman, sane for a moment, tugged a fallen beam from one of the guards and then fled into the hills. Many of the insane had to be rounded up from the area and brought back later.

On to the south the quake ran its race of destruction, ripping up railroad tracks, setting off landslides, destroying bridges, and smashing into the towns of Hollister, Santa Cruz, and Monterey. The force of the quake was lessening, but a final blow struck down the ancient mission of San Juan Bautista.

The fury of the earthquake was over now, although waves moved on as far as Los Angeles to rattle windows and make china dance.

In the desert to the south the shuddering earth rested at last, its final energy harmlessly spent in the sands.

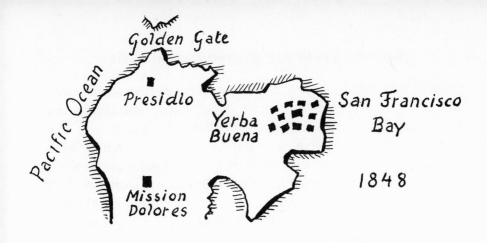

Golden Gate

Pacific Ocean

Presidio

Yerba Buena

San Francisco Bay

1848

Mission Dolores

3
Order from Chaos

In San Francisco the people crowding the streets began to come out of the shock of the first moments. But even as they gazed at shattered homes, they saw new danger.

San Francisco was on fire!

In the areas struck by the quake, gray wisps of smoke turned into yellow-black pillars tinged with red. Almost before the earthquake gave its last gasp, flames broke from the ruins. All over the city, snapped electric lines sent blue sizzles into rubble. Gas from broken pipes blazed. Sparks from heated chimneys and burning fuel ignited roofs or household furnishings. Kerosene from overturned lamps flared up. In a half hour fifty-two fires were reported, and many more must have been quenched by homeowners.

San Franciscans were proud of their city. Its history had begun in 1776, when the Spaniard Juan de Anza built a *presidio*, or fort, on the peninsula near the Golden Gate. The Spanish fathers erected Mission Dolores on the hills. Colonists came later to thrust up a few adobe huts and a trading post on a mudflat in a sheltered cove of the bay on the northeastern side of the peninsula. They named their settlement Yerba Buena and built it around a plaza, later called Portsmouth Square.

Mexico won independence from Spain in 1822. Under Mexican rule the village grew only slightly. A few more stores and a few more mud huts were added. American settlers moved in, and in 1848 the United States won California in the Mexican War. Yerba Buena became San Francisco.

The village had only 800 souls when gold was discovered in California in 1848. By the end of the year the muddy streets were thronged with more than 4,000 gold seekers. Businesses sprang up to dig a different kind of gold from prospectors. The Chinese came to work in the mines. Unsuited to such labor, thousands of Chinese moved to San Francisco to swell the growing population. They built Chinatown, with its narrow, colorful streets and alleys. They started laundries, restaurants, gambling dens, souvenir shops, and grocery stores.

The population of San Francisco actually grew in leaps. By 1860 the Comstock Lode in Nevada had been discovered, bringing silver prospectors and miners to the area. Mineowners built wealth for the city on the bay. That year saw the Pony Express carry the first mail from St. Louis to San Francisco. By 1869 the Central Pacific had joined its rails to the Union Pacific in Utah, and San Francisco had transcontinental railway service, although the line ended in Oakland across the bay. Later the Southern Pacific gave San Francisco a railroad terminus. The city rapidly became one of the major seaports on the West Coast.

The speed of San Francisco's growth was the cause of tragic destruction when fire followed earthquake in 1906. To meet the rapid increase in population, builders had used shoddy materials in hasty construction. Marshy ground had been carelessly filled, the houses on it built too close together. Chinatown and the area south of Market, with their flimsy wooden structures, were fire breeders. To be sure, some of the new skyscrapers and hotels were supposed to be fireproof, but most of the city's homes and buildings had been constructed of wood. Although wood resists earthquake shock better than brick, wood catches fire quickly.

Many citizens must have been aware of the peril to their city from fire that morning in April, but all had more present concerns. The cries of the injured and trapped had to be answered. Out of the first numbness of shock, some order began to grow. One man pulled at timbers pinning an injured person; others joined in the labor. Soon teams of rescuers were organized under the leadership of the most able among them. Wagons, carriages, and the city's few automobiles began to transport the seriously hurt to hospitals.

At the Emergency Hospital, doctors, nurses, and patients were pulled from the ruins. Patients were carried across the street to the Mechanics Pavilion, a huge sports arena. There a temporary hospital was set up to care for the earthquake victims.

Acting Fire Chief Dougherty took over for the injured Sullivan, and galloping horses soon pulled fire engines to spots of worst threat. Fires had to be reported by messenger, for all telephone lines were down. Firemen simply moved from one fire to the next worst blaze.

The men of Engine 38 were the first to make a dreadful discovery. South on Market they raced to a fire in a lodging house near the harbor. They screwed a hose into a hydrant and turned on the water. There came a trickle of muddy moisture. And then—nothing! There was no water in the mains. The earthquake had broken the pipes that led from reservoirs outside the city. There was water in the bay, and it could be pumped to fires near the harbor. There was water in old cisterns, dug in the early days. There was even usable moisture in the sewers. But

19

the firemen knew that, all told, these emergency sources would be only feeble aid in quenching the fast-spreading flames. Already several big fires were raging out of control.

Although there was little real panic among the people after the earthquake, the threat of fire brought confusion and growing turmoil. Refugees began to stream through the streets on their way to the safety of city parks. Chinese and Japanese rioted as they fought for standing room in Union Square. Thieves began looting deserted homes and buildings.

Two men that day acted quickly to put down the disorder and violence that was likely to follow disaster.

Mayor Eugene Schmitz, thrown from his bed by the first earthquake shock, dressed hastily and drove downtown in his carriage. All along the way he saw the havoc left by the quake. He saw the crush of people in the streets. He saw smoke and flame from many beginning fires. He knew that this disaster was the worst his city had ever known, and there had been many in its history—both earthquakes and fires. He faced the biggest task of his life.

Well over six feet tall, the mayor was a handsome man, with black hair and a dashing black beard. He had held his office for five years, years that had netted him a fortune in graft. Even now, powerful citizens were trying to bring him to trial for the mismanagement of civic funds. He was guilty and knew it. But this morning his only thought was for the welfare of his city. He had to bring order out of chaos.

He found the City Hall, where he had his office, in ruins and moved on to the Hall of Justice at Portsmouth Square. This building had been so badly damaged that its upper and ground floors were unsafe. Courage was needed to set up quarters in the dangerous basement, but Schmitz had courage that day. Since there was no electricity, he lit candles and went into conference with Chief of Police Dinan. Thousands were homeless, the chief

said, and more soon would be if the fires were not stopped. There was no water, and food supplies were short. Already there was rioting and looting. Saloons had been robbed of liquor.

Mayor Schmitz promptly ordered the police to close the thousand saloons in the city at once. He sent a telegram to the governor of the state asking for food and medical supplies. Another wire went to the mayor of Oakland across the bay: "SEND FIRE ENGINES, HOSE, ALSO DYNAMITE IMMEDIATELY."

At the suggestion of a businessman who came in, Schmitz appointed a Committee of Safety to plan for the welfare of the city. Named to the committee were fifty of San Francisco's wealthy and powerful men, some of whom were his worst enemies. They were to work with him on problems of health and sanitation, of keeping order in the disrupted city, of fighting fires. This done, Schmitz strode out to inspect the advance of the flames.

Another man was acting with the same speed, but without authority. He was the Commanding General of the U.S. Army's Department of California, Frederick Funston. He, too, had been spilled from his bed in his home on Nob Hill by the first earthquake shock. Getting into his uniform, he dashed out to view the damage. From the top of the hill he looked down on the tumbled buildings of the business district. He saw columns of smoke rising, saw the crowds in the streets. An Army man, he knew at once that soldiers would be needed to help police and firemen. There were soldiers at the Presidio and at Fort Mason, north toward the Golden Gate, but he could not order troops into the city on his own authority. He needed a request for aid sent from Mayor Schmitz to Secretary of War William Howard Taft.

General Funston was a man of quick thought and rapid action. He could see the skeleton of the ruined City Hall and knew that the mayor could not be working there. The best place to find him should be where the fire seemed worst—in the wholesale district. The general tried to thumb rides in passing cars, but drivers were too bent on sight-seeing to stop. Very well. He would walk.

At a fire on Sansome Street, a policeman said the mayor might be in the Hall of Justice. Again, he might not. Nobody knew. Funston had red hair, a fiery temper, and an adventuresome spirit. Certainly there was no time for red tape. If he could not get authority to order out troops, he would act on his own. Later he would face reprimand or court-martial if necessary. Turning on his heel, he stomped back across Nob Hill to the Army stables. He had breath enough to shout out an order.

"Saddle your horse," he told a young soldier. "Ride to Fort Mason. Bring back every engineer you can find."

Scribbling a note, he handed it to one of his aides with orders to ride with it to the officer in command at the Presidio.

"Send all troops," the note said briefly. "Report to the Chief of Police at the Hall of Justice."

The general looked at his watch. It was now six o'clock, less than an hour after the earthquake. Soldiers would be reporting to the police by seven. After mounting a horse, he rode down to Market Street. For the rest of the long day he was in the saddle, directing and encouraging his men.

In midmorning he remembered to send a telegram to Secretary Taft in Washington to report the disaster and the use of troops without authority. Funston concluded his message: "I SHALL DO EVERYTHING IN MY POWER TO RENDER ASSISTANCE AND TRUST THE WAR DEPARTMENT TO AUTHORIZE ANY ACTION I MAY HAVE TO TAKE . . . . WE NEED TENTS AND RATIONS FOR 20,000 PEOPLE."

Taft's reply, much delayed, read: "OF COURSE, DO EVERYTHING POSSIBLE."

Before the general's first message reached Washington, Funston wired again for an increase in supplies "FOR 100,000 PEOPLE." Still later he asked for "ALL AVAILABLE SUPPLIES."

The fires were spreading rapidly.

4

Wednesday Morning

San Francisco had 38 horse-drawn fire engines, 585 firemen, and 600 policemen. Seventeen hundred of Funston's soldiers were downtown early. But all the available forces and equipment could not stop the mad march of the blazes that had begun that morning.

By six o'clock great fires were burning out of control in two separate areas: north of Market in the wholesale and produce district between the waterfront and Sansome Street, and south of market from the harbor to Sixth Street. Both these sections had suffered severe earthquake damage, and fire spread rapidly in the rubble of toppled buildings.

South of Market the flames advanced a mile inward from the waterfront, racing from factory to factory, from one flimsy wooden shop or house to the next. There was no stopping the surge of fire that swallowed whole blocks and hurtled across streets to ignite other rows of closely crowded buildings. Firemen fought with every means at hand—water drawn in bathtubs at the time of the quake, water from cisterns and from watering troughs for horses, trickles from hydrants, even filth pumped from the sewers. But without water from the mains, they could not stop the wall of flame from raging southward. Arms of fire were also reaching northwest toward the business district on Market and Mission streets, where many of the city's finest buildings stood.

Aware that the area south of Market was doomed, the people who lived there fled their burning homes. Into the streets they poured, hurrying to seek the safety of parks or waterfront. They pushed before them or dragged behind them anything that could move on wheels—baby carriages, toy wagons, wheelbarrows, tables or sofas on casters, sewing machines. One family even tugged and heaved a piano. Trunks scraped on cobblestones or moved on roller skates nailed to the bottoms. Every makeshift cart was piled high with what people had snatched in haste— food, clothing, bedding, pots and pans. Women carried their babies or toted huge bundles on their backs. Frightened little children clutched beloved toys or pets and clung to the hands of struggling, laden parents.

Market Street was soon thronged with refugees. Policemen urged on the homeless in orderly streams. Soldiers kept the curious from the fire lines. Buggies and autos of sightseers clogged the street until the police took over vehicles to carry the wounded to emergency hospitals.

On the north side of Market, between Sansome Street and the bay, the dozen or so fires were turning into one huge fire. There, where many of the structures were of brick and mortar, the flames ate more slowly, destroying one building at a time. But even those that were supposedly fireproof could not long resist the terrific heat from a burning one next door. Firemen chopped away with axes and fought with blankets doused in whatever moisture could be found. Men were helpless, however, to stop even this slower advance of the flames.

This North of Market Fire was spreading in three directions—north toward Telegraph Hill, south to join the wall of flame across Market, and west toward the important financial district.

Flames jumped Sansome and began eating toward Montgomery Street, on which many of the city's banks were located. Bankers, tellers, and clerks, who had hurried downtown after the quake, began frenzied efforts to save the millions of dollars in currency, stocks, and bonds locked in the vaults.

Amadeo Giannini thought that his small Bank of Italy seemed well out of the path of the fire, but he took no chances. Loading the bank's funds on two wagons, he and a clerk drove to Giannini's home in nearby San Mateo. There the valuables were hidden behind the bricks of the fireplace.

Tellers from another bank dumped a million dollars into wheelbarrows and trundled them down Market to the harbor, where a boat was found to take the money across the bay to an Oakland bank.

Charles Crocker, of the Crocker-Woolworth Bank, loaded sacks and chests of money into wagons and drove, with the aid of a clerk, through clogged Market Street to the Ferry Building. Searching out Tom Crowley, a boatman who had a string of motor launches at one of the piers, Crocker hired a boat. He gave the driver instructions to take the money out into the bay and sit there with it until told to bring it in.

Crowley did a big business that morning and all during the disaster. Thousands of refugees rode to safety across the bay in his launches. The fare was fifty cents—"if you have it."

Draymen were not so reasonable in their charges. With wagons in demand by businessmen trying to save their records, drivers soon began charging $50 to $75 to carry a load.

Alice Eastwood, curator of botany for the California Academy of Sciences, was nearing fifty years of age, but she had strength for a big task that morning. Downtown early, she shoved against the stream of refugees until she reached her headquarters on Market. Earthquake had destroyed the stairs in the building, and fire was threatening it from the south. She had to save her famous collection of botanical specimens, housed on the sixth floor. The iron railing of the stairs was still intact. She climbed it, packed her specimens in bundles, lowered them to the first floor with ropes, climbed back down the railing, hired a wagon, and drove to a safe place. All that she saved for herself was the clothing she wore.

Other public-minded people were at work. The Sutro Library, with its valuable collection of rare books, was in the path of the flames threatening Montgomery Street. Workers loaded the volumes into wagons and drove across town to the Mechanics Pavilion, already in use as an emergency hospital. Ironically, the brick library building withstood the flames, but the pavilion later caught fire. The books had to be moved again.

Out to the west, beyond Van Ness Avenue, was Hayes Valley, a crowded district of homes. A woman whose apartment building had been severely damaged by the quake decided to get a breakfast of ham and eggs for her children. Unaware that the chimney was down, its flue damaged, she kindled a fire in her cookstove. Sparks from the flue set the walls afire. From the blazing apartment house, fire swept east toward Van Ness and the ruined City Hall. This new blaze came to be called the Ham and Eggs Fire.

Firemen, struggling to combat the South of Market Fire, looked up to see the huge cloud of smoke to the west from the Ham and Eggs Fire. If this new blaze leaped Market Street, they would be trapped between two raging sheets of flame.

Down on the waterfront, Marines and Navy men from the naval station on Mare Island saved the Ferry Building and its piers by hosing them with water from the bay. But they could not keep the flames from racing southward into the factory district and the old wooden buildings on the south side of Mission Street.

All during the earlier morning hours, workers had fought to contain the fires inside the two big areas south and north of Market. Just before nine o'clock, in spite of all efforts, the two huge fires joined across the northern end of Market, turning that section of the street into an inferno that kept refugees from reaching the Ferry Building.

Mayor Schmitz knew that something had to be done to halt the fire before it consumed the entire business district. Early that morning he had asked officers at the Presidio to send dynamite. But the Presidio had only black powder explosive. At Sansome Street, six wagons loaded with powder had arrived under the command of Lieutenant Briggs. Young Briggs knew that the powder was dangerous and would merely spread the fires.

"There is dynamite at Angel Island across the bay," he told the firemen. "Let us send for it and wait."

Back to the fight went the firemen. A battle began on Mission Street to save the huge United States Mint and the millions of dollars in coin and bullion locked in its vaults. Since it was built of stone and steel, the building was expected to resist fire. But heat from a burning shop next door blew out the windows, and fire was inside the mint. Firemen poured water from an indoor cistern on woodwork as it ignited and beat out blazes on the roof. The battle lasted seven hours, but the mint was saved.

Another Mission Street battle saved the Post Office. Clerks used wet mail sacks to beat out every fire that started inside. Later in the day, firemen dynamited nearby buildings to create a firebreak.

Other important buildings could not be saved. Burned to the ground was the Opera House, where Caruso had sung for a cheering audience the night before. With it went eight carloads

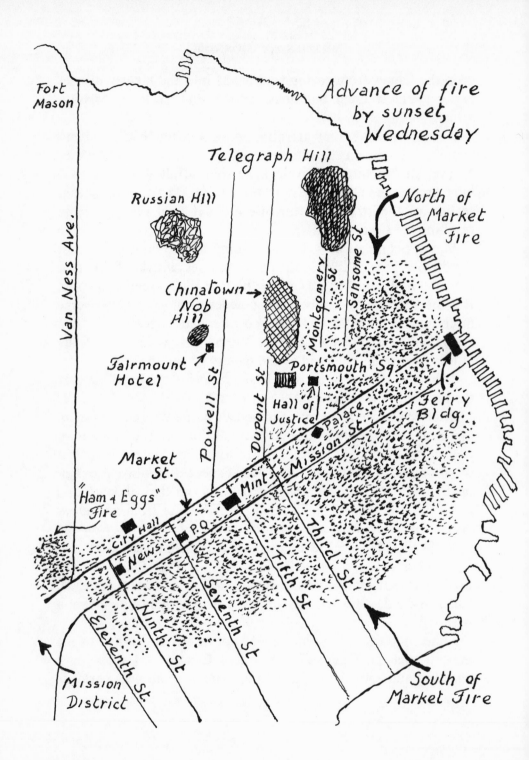

Advance of fire by sunset, Wednesday

Fort Mason

Telegraph Hill

Russian Hill

North of Market Fire

Van Ness Ave.

Chinatown
Nob Hill

Montgomery St

Sansome St

Fairmount Hotel

Powell St

Dupont St

Portsmouth Sq.

Hall of Justice

Ferry Bldg.

Market St.

Palace

Mint

Mission St

"Ham & Eggs" Fire

City Hall

P.O.

News

Eleventh St.

Ninth St.

Seventh St.

Fifth St.

Third St.

Mission District

South of Market Fire

of the Metropolitan's costumes. St. Patrick's Church, already injured by the quake, went up in flames.

The southern fire front soon reached into the business district along Market. The newspaper offices, the *Call* Building and the eighteen-story *Examiner* Building, turned into raging columns of flame. The Emporium, San Francisco's famous department store, was soon gone. Burned was the Academy of Sciences, from which Alice Eastman had rescued her botanical specimens.

Firemen ran from building to building, trying to beat out sparks and small blazes before big fires could start. Often they were close to death in smoke and flame and had to flee for their lives.

Policemen shoved back onlookers, carried the injured to ambulances, and drove looters away from store windows. Men, water, and equipment were in all too short supply to stop the conflagration.

Meanwhile, the Ham and Eggs Fire began eating its way from the west toward Van Ness Avenue and Market Street. St. Ignatius Church, with its beautiful murals and fine pipe organ, yielded to the flames. The Mechanics Pavilion was soon in danger.

Doctors and nurses, many of them slightly injured when the City Hall collapsed during the earthquake, had worked heroically to set up emergency treatment and operating space for surgery in the pavilion. They had handled thousands of cases of the maimed and burned, brought in by commandeered wagons and cars. Now smoke was filling the building. The roof was afire. Nurses seized children and carried them out. Doctors and orderlies shouted commands. Every patient who could walk lifted the seriously injured onto stretchers and staggered out of the burning building. Cars, wagons, ambulances clattered off to safety with the sick. Behind them the Mechanics Pavilion burst into flames.

Refugees still clogging Market now saw a ring of fire closing in on them. The stench of black smoke filled the air. Everywhere they saw the red of leaping flames. A river of people began flowing into side streets, herded on by policemen and soldiers. To squares and parks and hills the refugees fled, turning in dazed silence, when they were safe, to watch their city burn.

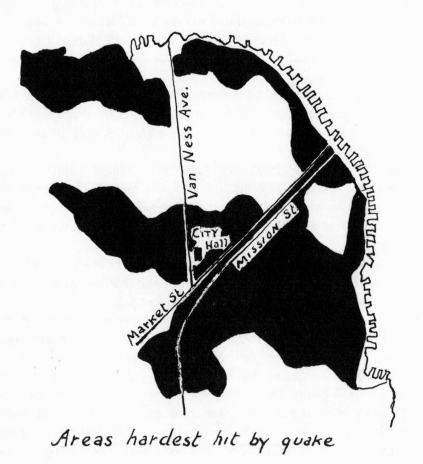

Areas hardest hit by quake

5

Wednesday Afternoon

The dynamite from Angel Island did not arrive until noon. Firemen tossed aside their useless hoses and prepared to blast buildings in the path of fires. Again Lieutenant Briggs protested to the mayor. Dynamiting would serve only to spread the fires faster, Briggs said, unless the charges were set off at some distance from the fire fronts and the debris from any destroyed area was cleared away before the flames could reach it. But Mayor Schmitz knew that owners would blame him for the demolishing of buildings not actually about to burn. He gave the order for the dynamiting to begin. Soon the dull boom of explosions was added to the crash of walls and the crackle of flames. Young Briggs was right: The rubble of the blasted buildings ignited rapidly, helping to start new blazes.

Schmitz, in the meantime, had turned to other problems. There are always mean and dishonest people who will see a chance in disorder for crime. All morning looters had been busy, breaking into shops to steal not only food, but also valuables. Steps had to be taken at once if a wave of crime were to be

33

stopped. Also, it was necessary to prevent householders from starting more fires such as the one triggered by the housewife in Hayes Valley.

The mayor called a meeting of the Committee for Safety and asked for suggestions. Although they did not like to work with him, the members realized that his concern was for the safety of the city. They told him their ideas. A proclamation to the citizens was drawn up and sent to a printshop beyond the fires. Since there was no electricity, men turned the heavy wheels of the press by hand. Five thousand copies were soon ready to be posted on the streets.

PROCLAMATION BY THE MAYOR

The Federal troops, the members of the Regular Police Force and all Special Police Officers have been authorized by me to KILL any and all persons found engaged in Looting or in the Commission of Any Other Crime.

I have directed all the Gas and Electric Lighting Co.'s not to turn on Gas or Electricity until I order them to do so. You may therefore expect the city to remain in darkness for an indefinite time.

I request all citizens to remain at home from darkness until daylight every night until order is restored.

I warn all citizens of the danger of fire from Damaged or Destroyed Chimneys, Broken or Leaking Gas Pipes or Fixtures, or any like cause.

Dated, April 18, 1906.   E. E. SCHMITZ, Mayor

Fire was now racing closer and closer to the Hall of Justice, and dynamite charges were being set in the block of shabby buildings to the rear. Thousands of chickens, crated in freight cars on a siding near a wholesale packinghouse, had been released. They fled, squawking, from the flames only to be

pursued by gleeful children from Telegraph Hill. Policemen warned the mayor that he and the committee must move for safety across the street to Portsmouth Square, where the police department was already setting up new quarters. There the committee members, with many a wary glance at the tons of dynamite and black powder piled in the little plaza, hastily finished their business. Before they adjourned, the square itself was no longer very safe, and men had begun to cart the explosives away to the Fairmont Hotel on Nob Hill, which was thought to be safe from the flames.

James Phelan, one of the committee, was the richest man in San Francisco. As he was getting into his car, a weary, laden woman, with two children clinging to her untidy skirts, approached him.

"How do I get to Jefferson Square, away from the fire?" she asked.

"Help the lady into the car," James Phelan told his chauffeur. "Drive us at once to the square."

The wealthiest that day could take time to help the troubled.

All morning the Palace Hotel on the south side of Market Street had resisted flames and heat from the blazing buildings around it. Its foundations were 12 feet thick, its walls and windows braced with steel. There was water in a generous cistern in its basement and in reservoirs on the roof. If any building in the city could live through fire, people thought, it would be the Palace.

The hotel employees had gone calmly about their morning's work, serving breakfast to the hungry, calming frightened guests gathered in the lobby. Among them Enrico Caruso, still complaining loudly against San Francisco, sat on his luggage. About noon the Metropolitan Opera Company managed to find a wagon to cart its singers out of the fire area.

"Give me Vesuvius in my native Italy," Caruso raged, climbing into the wagon with the others. "Better a volcano eruption than earthquake and fire. If I get out alive, I will never come back to San Francisco."

By one o'clock most of the guests had left. Firemen and hotel employees were working together now, dragging hoses through the halls, soaking down the walls of rooms, pouring water on the roof. Above the hotel the flag that floated there to tell the city that the Palace still stood was often hidden by swirling smoke.

At two o'clock fire from buildings at the rear sent flames sweeping against the upper walls of the hotel. Black smoke rolled through the halls. Windows shattered from the heat. Fire was inside the fireproof hotel. The water in its cisterns and reservoirs was exhausted. Firemen and workers gave up the battle and fled the terrific heat. Watchers on the hills caught a

36

last glimpse of the flag through the billowing smoke. The next instant the flag was gone. The sturdy Palace Hotel was at last in the grip of destroying flames.

Across the street was the postal telegraph office, the city's only remaining wire link with the outside world. All morning and into the afternoon, the chief operator had been laboring to send out a deluge of messages, official and personal. At 2:20 P.M., he sent his last message:

> The City practically ruined by fire. It's within half a block of us in the same block. . . . Fire all around us in every direction. . . . It's awful. There is no communication anywhere and entire phone system is busted. I want to get out of here or be blown up.

The postal telegraph wire went dead. San Francisco seemed cut off from the world.

In the early afternoon, dynamiting of buildings around the city's smaller newspaper offices had kept fire from the *Daily News*. Its offices were farther to the south on the other end of Market. Now, the *Daily News* began to burn.

Lieutenant Briggs had used the last charges of dynamite to blow up the buildings behind the Hall of Justice. Now there was nothing left but the black powder. Wagons began carting the dangerous stuff to spots where it was most needed. Again Briggs protested that the powder would be sure to spray out flames that would only start more fires. Ordered to use it anyway, he watched the soldiers under his command as they prepared to blast a drugstore across from Portsmouth Square. Not far away was Chinatown, its wooden houses trimmed with brightly painted decorations. In the houses and shops so closely crowded together lived thousands of Chinese and Japanese, who would be homeless if fire spread to their area. The explosion

37

came. Briggs sighed as he saw pieces of burning bedding hurtle from a window of the apartment above the drugstore. The flaming bits sailed across Kearny Street to land on roofs there. Buildings blazed up. The new fire began a march straight toward Chinatown.

Behind Briggs in Portsmouth Square, the last loads of powder were being carted away. Milling refugees were fleeing the park, dragging their possessions behind them. Soldiers were hastily burying in a shallow grave the unidentified dead that had been brought to the square from the city morgue. Policemen were starting prisoners from the city jail on a march toward Fort Mason. A pall of smoke lay over the historic little plaza that had been a haven to many during the day. Quiet and deserted after long activity, it awaited the fire. Not long after sunset the Hall of Justice burst into flames.

Up on Nob Hill, as the sun set behind smoke-filled air, thousands of refugees stood in shocked silence. Below them they could see the blackened ruins left in the wake of the three great fire fronts. The entire south side of Market Street lay smoldering. Beyond, in the whole southern area from the waterfront to Eleventh Street, only the Post Office and the mint stood unharmed. The black hulks and hollow shells of other buildings loomed through the smoke. To the east, the North of Market Fire had burned the financial district and was moving west toward Chinatown. The Ham and Eggs Fire was close now to the City Hall. Its flames had leaped Market and joined the southern fire, and together they were sweeping toward the Mission District, a place of closely crowded homes. To the watchers it seemed that the whole city was afire.

6
Night of Red Twilight

Night came to San Francisco, but not darkness. An eerie red glow lit the sky from the forty city blocks on fire, making night almost as bright as day. The red of leaping flames outlined the black clouds of smoke that rose high above the city. Ashes drifted down through air filled with the stench of burning.

In parks and vacant lots, from Union Square near Market to Fort Mason and the Presidio on the north and Golden Gate Park to the west, the 100,000 people who had left burning homes behind them found what small space they could. Piling their pitiful possessions around them, they made ready to spend the night. Some fortunate ones were taken into the homes generously opened to them throughout the western and northern residential districts all the way to the Pacific. Most of the homeless, however, camped in the parks or on the streets. They were joined by many whose homes had not been touched by fire, for everybody feared another earthquake. During the day there had been aftershocks. Who could know when another temblor might come?

39

Suppers were sketchy affairs of whatever food had been carried away from the fire in bundles or on improvised carts. But here and there, fireplaces were built of bricks from fallen chimneys so that coffee and hot food could be prepared.

Parents put children to bed on the ground, wrapping them in coats and sweaters or blankets, if any had been saved from the flames. Fathers tried to make shelters from clothing, sheets, or tarpaulins, propping up their makeshift tents with boards or pieces of furniture. Mothers rocked babies to sleep in their arms and held them so through the long hours.

All night long, refugees from newly dynamited or burned areas kept pouring westward. Space was hard to find. People slept under trees and bushes, in backyards, even on the rough cobblestones of the paving. They slept leaning against curbs and bits of furniture.

Many slept not at all. They watched the march of the fire or roamed from group to group, listening to the stories of escape, of loss, of death. Wild rumors spread rapidly, and tales of looting, crime, and disaster grew larger with each telling. Most of the rumors were completely false. San Francisco, some said, was not the only great city in the United States stricken. New Orleans had sunk under the Gulf of Mexico . . . Los Angeles was totally destroyed by the quake . . . Chicago was flooded by the waters of Lake Michigan . . . Portland and Seattle had been swept by tidal waves. San Francisco was said to be under martial law; soldiers had shot hundreds of looters without mercy.

It was true that some looters had been shot, but the number was small. The city had not been under martial law that Wednesday, nor was it ever to be in the days to come. Army officers had been careful to obey orders issued by the civil authorities.

Complaints about the activities of pickpockets were true enough. In streets crowded with hurrying refugees, sneaking

petty thieves, many of whom had hurried into the city when they heard the news of the disaster, had managed to have themselves a profitable day.

Many stories were told of the day's adventures. One young man had pushed his grandfather in a wheelchair through a blazing street. A husband and wife had buried their silverware in the garden and planned to return to dig up their valuables. A youth told of giving an expensively dressed woman a ride from one of the fire areas. Her hand was heavily bandaged. When he asked her how it had been hurt, she showed him how she had wrapped her jewels under the cloth to keep them safe from thieves.

The story was told of how soldiers had been stopped from dynamiting the Montgomery block, east of the Hall of Justice. At a window had appeared the startling figure of a religious fanatic, Elder Treadwell, with his long, flowing white hair and beard. Leaning out, he had foretold woe to any man who dared to destroy "the Ark of the Lord." Frightened by the curses laid upon them, the soldiers had turned away. Saved from dynamiting, the Montgomery block resisted fire.

Many of the homeless were sad and frightened, but San Franciscans came largely from the sturdy stock that had settled the West. Their forebears had crossed the plains, climbed the mountains, and fought their way over the burning deserts. They had battled hostile Indians. They had braved the dangers of the sea to come round Cape Horn. They had begun the building of the beautiful city on the bay. Fire and earthquake and the loss of all possessions would not keep the sons and grandsons of pioneers from picking up the shattered pieces of their lives and going bravely on. When the fires were over, the people said, they would build the city again.

Jack London, the famous author of many books and stories about the West, such as *The Call of the Wild*, had hurried to San

Francisco from his home in Sonoma County at the first news of the disaster. Later he wrote: "Never in all San Francisco's history, were her people so kind and courteous as on this night of terror."

He was right. Those who had been wise enough to bring food gave to the less fortunate. Children without shelter were put to bed under the makeshift tents of other parents. The sick and the aged were given gentle care. The wealthy shared with the poor, the poor with the rich.

Some could even laugh over their troubles. They smiled at the way people were dressed—or undressed, for many still wore nightclothes or long underwear. Young people danced to the gay music of an accordion. One man had managed to save a piano from his home. Before the night was over, a crowd gathered around it to listen to the music, and two girls climbed up to sit atop the piano and sing, with grim humor, "There'll be a hot time in the old town tonight."

For those who battled the fire all night there was, indeed, a "hot time in the old town." Firemen, policemen, soldiers, sailors, and Marines fought a losing struggle against the advancing flames through all those desperate hours.

For a time after sunset the wind, which had blown steadily all day, died down a little. Then it came again, this time veering from direction to direction. The weary fighters had hoped for the usual night fog to damp the fires down, had hoped for rain. But neither fog nor rain drifted in from the sea that night.

The Ham and Eggs Fire had been somewhat controlled shortly after dark. But soon it flared up again to find new fuel in the ruined City Hall, destroying the 85,000 books of the Public Library on the second floor and burning the city records in the offices. Raging across Market to the south, it sent a fiery arm into the Mission District, with its closely crowded homes.

In the South of Market area, the fire had been halted at

43

Folsom Street, but early in the evening it jumped that street and swung on southward. Fire roared down Third Street to attack the Southern Pacific depot and the railroad yards. A few firemen and employees, left to guard the empty building, fought a long and valiant battle with one thin stream of water, pumped from the bay, and with wet sacks. The fight lasted into the night, but the depot, through which tons of supplies would reach the city in the next few days, was saved.

All through the day, fire fighters had made various stands as the fires progressed, retreating only when a street seemed doomed. They were concentrating now on Powell Street, moving fire engines and equipment there to have in readiness for a desperate effort to keep the north and south fires from joining the Ham and Eggs front approaching from the southwest. If the three fronts united, flames would sweep on to consume the whole western area.

Powell Street, by its very width, offered a natural firebreak. Then, too, on its east side was Union Square, a long block of grass and trees that might serve as another firebreak. Directly across the street from the square was the huge St. Francis Hotel, which surely could resist heat and flame. Along Powell in the four blocks before it reached Nob Hill, there were scattered vacant lots that would be helpful. The new stand seemed a wise choice, especially since the firemen had time to prepare a fighting line.

They hooked their hoses into wells and sewer lines, piled wet blankets handy, and placed shovels and pickaxes along the street. Policemen and soldiers ordered all remaining residents to leave the area. When all was in readiness, the exhausted men dropped down on curbs and lawns to snatch a few minutes of needed rest.

A group of tired soldiers, while they waited, decided to brew a pot of coffee in the vacated Delmonico, a famous French restaurant a block east of Union Square. Against orders, they lighted a campfire. It blazed up, and the whole building caught fire before they could control the flames, which spread too rapidly.

In the meantime, the fire in the financial district, which had died down somewhat, suddenly blazed up again. Earlier in the day, it had skipped a block that contained the Brooklyn Hotel. The hotel's residents had returned toward evening to find their rooms still livable, although the walls were hot to the touch. Thankful not to have to spend the night in the streets, they had moved back in. Now the building exploded into flames, and again they fled.

On the north side of Market Street, across from the burned *Examiner* and *Call* offices, the building that housed the last of the city's great newspapers, the *Chronicle*, had withstood heat and flames. Now its roof caught fire. The upper story, where the linotype machines stood, burned. The machines crashed down through seven floors. Fire followed, to leave the *Chronicle* Building only a black shell.

The fire in the financial district joined forces with the Delmonico Fire and swept down on the already-threatened Chinatown.

Many San Franciscans thought that Chinatown should have been destroyed long since. In its twelve blocks of colorful, crowded streets and narrow alleys lived 25,000 Chinese and Japanese, some very wealthy, many extremely poor. The area had many respectable businesses—souvenir shops, cafés, laundries, grocery stores. But there were also many gambling and opium dens. There were dark cellars in which hundreds of Chinese lived, crammed together in utter poverty.

Now Chinatown was doomed. As flames raced through the flimsy wooden buildings, thousands of Chinese fled to nearby Union Square, up Nob and Russian hills, or down to the harbor. Long queues swaying down their backs, the men led little children by the hand. The women tottered painfully along on tiny, bound feet in three-inch soles. Behind them Chinatown was soon a red furnace. By midnight this colorful, sinful section of San Francisco was a smoldering pile of ashes.

In Union Square thousands of sleepless refugees watched the fire begin to encircle their safe block of trees and grass. From the north, south, and east, sparks lit on roofs of homes and shops surrounding the square. The roofs smoldered in smoke for a moment and then burst into red flame.

"The Lord sent it! The Lord sent it!" a half-crazed man began to shout.

Soldiers quieted him and ordered people to leave the park. In a disordered wave the refugees were on the run again. Loaded with bundles, they went, dragging furniture and trunks behind them, tugging along their children. To the still-safe west they moved, hoping to find another haven.

One side of the square had not begun to burn. Here stood the sturdy St. Francis Hotel to act as a firebreak if the flames should jump Powell Street. The firemen still believed that a stand on the street might work. But at one o'clock the spire of a church blazed up, sending fiery embers across Powell into an area of wooden homes built close together. From the east the Delmonico Fire spread across Powell, and the supposedly fireproof St. Francis ignited. Soon every building on the fourth side of the square was ablaze.

The Powell Street stand was a failure!

In the red-swept hours before dawn, the weary fire fighters began moving their scarred and blackened equipment to Nob Hill, where they planned to make another desperate stand. If the line of fire could not be halted there, the entire northwestern residential district must yield to the merciless flames.

7

Smoke-Dark Morning

Thursday, April 19, was blessed with California sun, but the exhausted fire fighters and the 200,000 homeless people did not feel its warmth or see its brightness. Over the city hung dense clouds of yellow-black smoke that rose two miles into the air.

Watchers on the now-threatened hills could see the progress the fire had made during the night. The entire business district was gone. All the remaining buildings on the north side of Market, even the solid new Flood Building with its walls of granite, had burned before dawn. Only blackened, smoking hulks were left on both sides of the great diagonal street. The area south of Market was a ruin of rubble and ashes, so demolished that it was scarcely possible to see where streets had been. To the southeast a sheet of flame was rocketing into the Mission District, where laborers and middle-class workers had their homes. The northern wholesale and retail district was a mass of reeking rubble.

Fire was still marching on. It was spreading slowly against a strong wind toward Telegraph and Russian hills. Waves of fire

47

were racing toward Nob Hill, so named because on its crown the railroad barons and the silver kings—the nabobs—had built their mansions.

Leland Stanford, one of the four men who had built the western half of the transcontinental railroad, had been the first one to choose this commanding sight above the city. He had bought a two-acre lot, surrounded it with a huge stone wall, and built within it a mansion. Its entrance hall had an inlaid black marble floor and was lit by a glass dome 70 feet above.

Mark Hopkins, another of the railroad four, was a quiet, thrifty man, unimpressed by his great wealth. For years he had lived in a modest cottage, rented for $35 a month. Known to many as "Uncle Mark," he had been happy spending his leisure hours raising vegetables in his backyard. His wife had different ideas concerning the uses of wealth. She had argued him into building a monstrous castle, adorned with turrets and towers, gables and bay windows. One of the bedrooms was lined with ebony and set with gems. The dining room seated sixty, although the Hopkins had no children and seldom entertained guests. Uncle Mark thought the palace a big joke and referred to it laughingly during its construction as the Hotel de Hopkins. He had never lived in it, dying before its completion.

Of the other two railroad barons, Charles Crocker had built a wooden monstrosity, with a 76-foot tower, and Collis Huntington had been satisfied with a large but unornamented Georgian house.

The money kings were gone by the time of the fire, their elaborate castles empty or used by public institutions. San Franciscans thought the buildings ugly, but they were proud of them just the same.

"After all," many said, "they have their uses."

In 1906 the Stanford house was used as San Francisco headquarters for Stanford University. Mrs. Hopkins' dream home had become the Hopkins Art Institute, managed by the University of California. In its splendid rooms were displayed paintings and statuary valued at thousands of dollars. Now the gallery was in the path of the fire.

During the night faculty and students of the institute, joined by a band of students from the University of California, had worked to carry paintings and statues out to the lawns in front, carting away as many as they could in wheelbarrows to safer places. At eight in the morning fire reached the institute. Flames attacked the west wing, after first consuming the Stanford home. Bystanders joined the students in hastily transferring the art treasures across the street to the lawns of the Flood mansion.

As all worked furiously, the fire swept around the Fairmont Hotel and set the Flood mansion ablaze. A University of California professor cut as many paintings as he could from their frames, rolled them up, and fled with them under his arm. Later he took them to the university. With him in flight went soldiers, sailors, firemen, and volunteers, for the whole east side of Nob Hill was now burning lustily. The paintings left on the Flood lawn were destroyed by fire, as were the statues too large to be carried. Gone were the homes of the money kings, the mansions that had been part of San Francisco's skyline for many years.

Burned also was the stately new Fairmont Hotel, still under construction. It was being built of marble, cement, and stone, and firemen had hoped that it would resist heat and flame. But workmen had left paint and varnish piled in one room. Heat ignited the varnish; it exploded, turning the building into a column of flame. Mayor Schmitz and the police department had already deserted their headquarters in the Fairmont as the fire had advanced on Nob Hill.

Below the hill, the blaze that had jumped Powell Street the night before was swooping southward toward Van Ness Avenue. In the blocks ahead of the approaching sheet of flame, people

gathered in the streets to mill about in confusion. Grocers opened their doors and told people to take what they could carry. Wealthy women, wearing their fur coats and jewels to save them, elbowed into the line with poorly dressed women. All snatched what they could. Some dumped their loads with relatives or friends and went back for more. One grocer refused to open his store, even when the fire was only a block away. Angry shouts came from the crowd.

"Open up and let us in!"

"You can't save anything, anyway!"

A soldier on guard against looters saw the crowd break down the door and rush in. He allowed them to enter.

"Everything's going to burn," he told the grocer. "Let them have it. They all need food."

Through wide Van Ness Avenue the new homeless poured in a crush like the one that had clogged Market the day before. Deafening noise added to the confusion. Autos honked for passage, dynamite blasts boomed, and the terrifying sound of crackling flames surged nearer. Horse-drawn drays, hand-pushed carts of all kinds, men, women, and children—all tried to shove a way to safety. Everybody carried huge bundles. One group had loaded its possessions on a long ladder with rollers underneath.

In two directions the refugees fled, some east toward burned out Market Street, some west around the fire. Many headed toward the ferries, hoping to find a way out of the city.

The Ferry Building and the piers, saved from fire on the first day, were scenes of disorder. Thousands, clamoring for boat passage, crowded the waiting rooms and overflowed into the street. Seventy people a minute were leaving the city, but even that speed was not enough to thin the crowds.

Enrico Caruso shoved his way through the lines. The Metropolitan had finally found a launch to carry away its singers, and

Caruso raged when policemen guarding the gates would not let him through to the pier. The great tenor, angry at not being recognized, brandished his autographed photograph of President Theodore Roosevelt in their faces.

"See! See!" Caruso shouted. "The President's picture! Autographed to me—Caruso!"

The policemen shrugged and let the enraged man through to the waiting launch. A story has it that the tenor shook his fist at the city as the boat pulled away. He kept his resolve never to return. San Francisco had seen the last of Enrico Caruso.

In spite of the growing disorder in the city, there were many cool-minded, public-spirited people at work.

Papa Coppa, whose restaurant had not burned, had plenty of food, but he dared not build a fire inside his café. Lugging a large piece of mutton to burned-out Portsmouth Square, he built a campfire, made a huge pot of stew, and served it free to refugees.

Mrs. Merrill, head of the San Francisco Red Cross, hung a Red Cross flag above her beautiful home on Van Ness and opened her doors to the hungry, feeding all that came.

The Post Office staff began handling mail. Without available telegraph service, mail was doubly important. Messages to relieve the minds of worried relatives poured in. Many of the notes were written on scraps of paper, cardboard, or newspaper, even on char-bordered shingles. Postage was not demanded. If the letter had an address, it was sent.

An extra hit the streets on Thursday morning. With the great newspaper buildings destroyed, reporters and editors from three papers had crossed the bay to Oakland. They had the biggest scoop of their lives—the destruction of a great city by earthquake and fire. They had been there. They had seen disaster. And they wanted to get their story to the world. Forgetting that

52

they were employees of rival newspapers, they banded together to put out a combined *Call-Chronicle-Examiner* extra. All night they had worked, running off the result of their efforts on the presses of the Oakland *Tribune*.

Hastily prepared by exhausted men, many of whom were worried about the safety of their families, the four-page paper held many statements that were untrue. But under a two-line scare heading—EARTHQUAKE AND FIRE: SAN FRANCISCO IN RUINS—the little paper told the story of the biggest disaster that had ever hit the United States. San Franciscans bought it eagerly or were given a copy if they had no dime to pay for it. The extra was news. It was also the result of the courage, determination, and dedication of newsmen.

Fiery, red-bearded little General Funston had never stopped his efforts to bring order to the city. All during the day and night Wednesday, he had ridden his horse from fire line to fire line, making his headquarters on the streets where he could. On Thursday morning he moved his quarters to Fort Mason on the bay end of Van Ness. Knowing that soldiers were desperately needed, he sent out orders for more to come from every military establishment not too far away. In charge of all the military forces, he assigned parts of the city to each force under the command of a reliable officer.

Funston knew that water was another big necessity, both for drinking and for fighting fire. To Mare Island he sent a message asking for a supply of fresh water to be sent. Orders also went to the superintendent of the city's water system to find all available sources of water within San Francisco—lakes, creeks, springs, cisterns, wells.

The general had already sent a second telegram to the War Department through the Oakland wires. He had asked for tents and food for 100,000 homeless people. Now he sent a third telegram:

. . . Impossible now to inform you as to full extent of disaster. City practically destroyed. Troops have been aiding police and maintaining order. Martial law has not been declared. . . . You cannot send too many tents or rations. About 200,000 homeless. Food very scarce. Provision houses all destroyed. All government buildings in city gone.

Mayor Schmitz also had been up all night. With his headquarters in the Fairmont burned, he called a morning meeting of the Committee for Safety in a dance hall near Van Ness. His clothes were wrinkled and soiled, and his face was drawn into lines of worry and exhaustion; but he still gave the impression of strength and courage. He was brief and tough. The homeless must have food and shelter. Epidemics must be prevented.

The men who had come to the meeting were discouraged, but he drove them without mercy, appointing committees to carry out his orders. They were to seek volunteers to collect every bit of food in the city. Wagons were to go to towns in the south and boats to cross the bay to bring back flour and other provisions. San Francisco bakeries that had escaped fire but were without electricity must somehow be put into operation so that they could start baking bread for the hungry. Supplies—food, medicines, disinfectants—were to be distributed to all the homeless in the parks and squares. Tents and cots, blankets and clothing must be found. Shelters had to be built. A grim order went to one committee—to see that all the dead were buried before pestilence could start.

Although many of these men hated Schmitz, they agreed to carry out his orders. He looked at them, sat back in his chair, and glanced at his watch. It was noon. He was about to explode a bombshell that would be certain to bring rebellion.

8

Desperate Fighting

Mayor Schmitz was grimly determined to enforce his will against all opposition. He knew too well the evil strength of the conflagration that was ravaging so many areas of the city.

Joined together in a solid mass of flame, the South of Market and the Ham and Eggs fires were eating deep into the Mission District. Although firemen were fighting the flames there from block to block, they were being forced back along a wide front. The North of Market Fire was the most to be feared because it threatened the destruction of much valuable property. It was well across Powell Street now and raging westward in a six-block line toward Van Ness Avenue.

Schmitz had decided before the meeting that the fire had to be stopped at Van Ness. Beyond the avenue to the west lay the Western Addition, a residence district of 150,000 people. Add that many to those already homeless, and San Francisco could never handle its enormous problem of providing food and shelter.

During the first day and night of the fire, Schmitz had refused to allow the blasting of buildings not certain to be burned. Now he had come to realize that young Briggs was right: The only way to halt the march of fire was to dynamite the blocks well in advance of a fire line so that the rubble of the blasting could be cleaned up before flames could attack.

Speaking slowly, he declared that Van Ness was to be the next stand made against fire. The avenue was 125 feet wide. The line of defense would stretch all the way to Fort Mason at the Golden Gate. He paused a moment and then exploded his bombshell.

"Gentlemen, I mean to order all buildings on the east side of Van Ness dynamited."

Startled gasps came from the members of the committee. On Van Ness were many of the finest homes in the city, even some belonging to these men. Angry protests began. He could not blow up the Van Ness mansions. There were splendid apartment houses there too, as well as homes and beautiful churches. He simply could not dynamite on Van Ness until fire actually reached each building. How could he know but that some of them might be saved?

The mayor was tough. Again he explained that the width of the avenue, added to the dynamiting on its east side, would form a barrier that the flames could not leap. Besides, what else was there to do?

This question the men could not answer. They knew in their hearts that the fire had to be halted on Van Ness or the whole city would burn. Grudgingly they yielded before the mayor's determination.

Schmitz went into action at once. Turning to Colonel Morris, whom General Funston had placed in command of some of the soldiers, and to Acting Fire Chief Dougherty, the mayor explained his plan and gave his orders. Blasting was to be stopped in other fire areas and all available dynamite brought at once to Van Ness Avenue. A boat was to be sent across the bay to bring more explosives to swell the nearly exhausted stores. Firemen that could be spared elsewhere were to gather at the avenue. Soldiers would begin ordering people out of homes and stores between the fire and Van Ness. The two men nodded and hurried away.

In his carriage Schmitz drove to Van Ness and waited for the fighting forces to arrive. In thirty minutes they began to straggle in from other parts of the city. Weary firemen, with blackened faces and eyes red-rimmed. Soldiers who had not slept since their arrival in the city on Wednesday morning. Worn-out horses, tugging grimed fire engines that had seen too much use. The firemen went doggedly to work, fitting hoses to hydrants, hunting cisterns and wells, preparing fire engines to pump filth from the sewers. When the work was done, the men dropped to the ground to await the arrival of the dynamite. Many fell at once into the dead sleep of utter exhaustion.

In the meantime, soldiers had been going from house to house in the blocks between the fire and Van Ness. Protesting people, ordered from their homes or shops, began pouring into Van Ness—another wave of refugees, loaded with what belongings could be snatched in haste. All were bewildered, and many were angry. They complained that the soldiers had not given them enough time to gather food and bedding together. Why must they go? The fire had not yet reached their homes. Perhaps it would turn in some other direction. And even if it didn't, they might be able to save their own homes from the flames.

When the doomed blocks were emptied, the soldiers began to ring doorbells on the east side of Van Ness. The people who lived there were rich, many of them millionaires. They reacted in various ways to the order to vacate. Some argued angrily against leaving their beautiful homes. One man even turned a pistol on the soldier at the door. The soldier merely pushed the pistol aside and forced the family to leave. For the most part, however, homeowners responded with courtesy, going without a backward look at their beloved possessions. Some joined the wave of refugees moving to the west, but many waited across the avenue, hoping that their homes might be spared both dynamite and fire.

Mrs. Merrill, whose mansion was full of treasures collected abroad, came to her door under its Red Cross banner, nodded with cool composure, and asked how long before she must leave.

"Thirty minutes," the soldier said.

"Thirty minutes will give me time to feed these people," she responded, waving a hand toward the crowd of refugees in her house.

It was three o'clock in the afternoon. The blocks to be dynamited had been emptied. Soldiers and firemen were ready for their stand on Van Ness. But the dynamite had not come!

The waiting men had no way of knowing that the mayor's order had not been carried out, perhaps because of the confusion on the docks. The boat had never left the pier. Lieutenant Briggs learned this fact and informed General Funston. The two officers hurried to the waterfront, pushing their way through the crush of people on the pier. The tug *Slocum,* loaded with refugees, was about to set out for Oakland. Funston ordered people off the boat and sent it across the bay to find dynamite.

In places the fire had now advanced to within a block of Van Ness. Fire fighters dared wait no longer for the dynamite. Flames were beginning to flare up in the very homes and shops that were to have been blasted to form a massive firebreak.

"Set fire to the buildings between the fire and Van Ness," someone suggested.

The decision to do so was quickly made. Soldiers ran from house to house with dishes of kerosene to set blazes. They broke windows with stones to create drafts that would encourage fire. When the buildings were burning well, firemen worked desperately to put out the flames and leave only blackened masses.

They hoped that the charred rubble might serve to halt the fast-nearing wall of fire from the east. The plan proved worse than useless. Soon five blocks on the east side of Van Ness were ablaze.

The fire on Nob Hill had spread down and into the streets that lay between the hill and Van Ness. In desperation firemen tried to stop it from reaching the avenue by blowing up houses in the blocks just before Van Ness. All they had to use was black powder, and as houses were blasted, they burst into flames. Soon the whole east side of Van Ness was on fire.

Firemen moved their engines and began a battle to keep the fire from leaping the avenue to its west side. At one place it did —for a time. In the steeple of St. Mary's Church, heat started flames that reached upward toward the cross at its top. Two heroic priests, Father O'Ryan and Father Ramm, climbed the steep steps inside the steeple. They risked their lives to climb a ladder under the great copper bell, aware that its moorings might give way at any moment and crush them in its fall. With the axes they had carried with them, they chopped away at the burning holes in the roof until they had put out all the blazes.

Firemen could get only thin streams of water from cisterns and sewage. The heat from the burning homes was so intense that any moisture merely turned to steam before it could reach the flames. Men fought a vast wall of fire. High above, pigeons flew away from smoke and flame.

Unable to endure the heat, the fire fighters fell back. If the east side of Van Ness was gone, perhaps they could save the west side of the avenue. But the heat was there, too. Showers of sparks fell on hands and faces and burned holes in clothing. Windows in homes on the west side shattered. Roofs and porches began to smolder.

The homeowners who had been waiting on the west side joined in the struggle to save their homes. They beat out starting blazes with wet coats and blankets dipped in buckets and bathtubs of water drawn at the time of the earthquake. With axes they chopped off burning shingles and flung them to the ground. All effort was useless. The fire was across Van Ness in a six-block arrowhead of smoke and flame. Soon it would rage on into the Western Addition.

Not until six o'clock did the dynamite arrive. Firemen shouted angrily at the wagon drivers that they had come too late, but Army and fire officers shoved away toward the dynamite wagons.

"Drive a block west to Franklin Street," they ordered. "We'll try a new stand there."

Again families were hastily ordered out. Charges of dynamite were set, and the booms of blasting rose into the smoke-filled air. Although the firemen felt sure that this new effort was useless, they fought the flames with dogged courage, using any moisture they could find—in cisterns, wells, and sewers, or hoarded bathtub water.

All night the weary men battled to keep the fire from jumping Franklin from the dynamited rubble on its east side. At midnight hope replaced despair. Dimly they realized that they had a chance to win. In one place the flames had been held back for a time by the wide lawns of the Spreckels estate, although the interior of the house burned. The wind, which had kept veering from direction to direction all day, began to blow steadily from the west. It served to hold back the fire. There was even a full head of water coming from one hydrant. Day long, night long efforts to repair the broken pipes from the city reservoirs were beginning to bring results.

But even as hope was born, a house on the west side of Franklin flared into flames. Firemen redoubled their efforts at that point. The fire was put out. Dynamiting and a few vacant lots kept the flames from spreading.

By dawn the weary firemen knew that they had won a victory. The six-block arrowhead of fire had been stopped at narrow Franklin Street. There was still fire, but everywhere it was dying down.

During that second day and night of red calamity, workers in the Mission District were also fighting a brave battle against flames. The Ham and Eggs Fire, spreading southward, was consuming home after modest home in an area five blocks wide. The Southern Pacific Hospital burned soon after its patients, including the dying Fire Chief Sullivan, had been removed to the Presidio.

On the fire surged, ravaging Thirteenth Street, Fourteenth, Fifteenth. At Sixteenth, workers made a heroic effort to fend old Mission Dolores from the flames. Built of adobe in the mission days of California's history, it was one of the oldest buildings in the city. It had been dedicated to St. Francis, and it was for that saint that San Francisco had been named. Forming a bucket line to carry water from a nearby pool, firemen managed to save the ancient church.

The fire had reached Nineteenth Street by midnight. Flames swept the Youth's Directory there, maintained by priests for homeless boys. The hundreds of boys who lived there were hurried into the hills to join the thousands of new refugees from the Mission area.

Houses had been dynamited all along Twentieth Street. Now firemen made a stand there. There were pools and springs at the top of a steep hill nearby, and water meant hope. The firemen tried to urge the exhausted horses into tugging the fire engines up the grade. Like the men, the horses had been working too many hours without sleep. The gallant animals responded to reins and shouts, but they did not have enough strength left to pull the heavy machines up the grade. Slowly the engines started to slide downhill, pulling the horses after them. Instantly, from the crowd of spectators, men, women, and children sprang forward. They manned ropes. They tugged and pushed the fire engines up the hill to the springs. With water in the hoses and the wind from the west helping, the firemen held back the flames.

Some time after midnight the Mission Fire was halted!

9

Help for the Homeless

San Francisco seemed to be cut off from the world, but news of the disaster was going out over the Oakland wires. People who had fled the city were telling their stories in California towns. The letters written on bits of paper and cardboard were reaching relatives and friends. Newspapers all over the country were flashing their stories to the world. Often their accounts were exaggerated, their statements sometimes false. But the nation and the world knew about the catastrophe. The response was generous.

When General Funston's first telegram had arrived Wednesday noon in Washington, Secretary of War Taft had called at the White House to talk with President Theodore Roosevelt. A message was sent to Congress asking for $500,000 to aid the stricken city. At once the sum was granted. Not long after the passage of the appropriation, the sum was doubled to $1,000,-000. When later telegrams came, Secretary Taft ordered Army rations for 200,000 people and tents for 20,000.

Soldiers, sailors, Marines, and men of the Coast Guard and

state militia were pouring into San Francisco to help keep order, prevent crime, handle the dynamite blasting, and fight fire. On Thursday evening the flagship of the Pacific Squadron, the *Chicago*, steamed into port at Fort Mason after a hasty trip from San Diego, and more Marines and Navy men reported for duty to General Funston. Troops, as well as needed supplies, were ordered down from Vancouver Barracks.

The state of California acted promptly in sending aid to the fire-stricken city. As soon as news of the earthquake reached Governor George C. Pardee, he had hurried to Oakland to set up an office from which to handle relief work. To Los Angeles he had sen an urgent telegram: "FOR GOD'S SAKE, RUSH ALL AVAILABLE FOOD TO SAN FRANCISCO AS SOON AS POSSIBLE. I WILL SEE THAT TRAINS ARE RUSHED THROUGH."

Los Angeles sent tons of food and medical supplies, also doctors and nurses and two carloads of bottled water. From Sacramento, the state capital, came riverboats loaded with provisions. The food was dumped on the dock, and the boats turned to aiding with the task of carrying refugees across the bay. Oakland opened its doors to the homeless and sent thousands of gallons of milk across the bay for babies and children. The city of Stockton used money set aside for its Fourth of July celebration to buy 8,000 eggs, hard-boil them, and deliver them to San Francisco along with a boatload of other food.

By Friday morning some of this help had already reached the city; more was on its way by boat or train. Help was desperately needed. Many of the refugees were without food, shelter, or adequate clothing. Their number had increased. In Golden Gate Park alone there were 200,000. Thousands more were crowded together on the grounds of the Presidio and Fort Mason. Nobody knew how many more were camped in every small park and vacant lot outside the fire areas.

Food was the greatest need. Many had eaten no decent meal since the night before the earthquake, and all were hungry. Soldiers began handing out Army rations that had come from Vancouver Barracks. Relief committees distributed what could be found or taken in town. Mayor Schmitz, who had insisted on enforcing the strict rule against looting, now gave soldiers and policemen orders to force grocers and butchers to give up their supplies. Thousands of pounds of half-cooked beef were discovered in a burned wholesale market. Bakeries outside the fire zones baked thousands of loaves of bread to add to those sent by Los Angeles housewives.

Rich and poor stood in long lines to wait for a handout of a few crackers, a couple of cans of food, or a loaf of precious bread. Women with babies might be lucky enough to get condensed milk. Money would buy little in the ravaged city. True wealth was a frying pan or cooking pot saved from a burning home. Utensils were used and passed on, lent again and again. Refugees who had thought to put can openers in their bundles were busy. Those who had managed to gather a few bricks for outdoor cooking pits turned them into community kitchens. Rich women in silk dresses waited in line beside housewives in bedraggled cottons for the privilege of warming the doled food. Hunger brought high and low to one level.

In the parks and squares and vacant lots, life went on, although there was great confusion everywhere. Some could only sit, bewildered, on their piled belongings while they ate the cold food given them. Others found relief in activity. Men went off to search in the rubble of ruined buildings for provisions of any kind or tried to build makeshift tables and chairs out of scraps of wood from the ruins. Mothers amused their children by playing games with them. In the flight from burning homes, families had been separated, and now parents searched for children, and husbands hunted for wives. Doctors hung out charred shingles

with the scrawled information that they were ready to treat patients. Bedding was hung on pieces of rope to dry, and mattresses were laid over boxes to air in the sun. On the streets past the parks, autos chugged, carrying such signs as AMBU- LANCE. RELIEF FOOD. NURSES. DOCTORS. MESSENGER.

Over the city still hung a pall of black smoke. But early on Friday morning, refugees began to tell each other hopefully that the smoke seemed a little less dense. Word soon began to spread that the fire had been controlled in the Mission District and stopped at Franklin Street. Could the fires be over at last?

But even as they gazed and wondered, they knew that San Francisco faced another day of fire, another flight from flames. True, the smoke to the south had thinned, but new black columns, tinged with red, were rising high into the air in the northwest.

10
The Last Battles

The west wind had helped to halt the six-block fire front at Franklin Street in the small hours of Friday morning. But by dawn the fire fighters knew that the wind had brought as much calamity as it had blessing. The fire behind them, raging westward from Nob Hill during the night, had not crossed Van Ness on its northern reaches. But the flames, unable to leap the broad avenue, had turned back and swept to the north and east, fanned by the eastward-blowing wind. The concentration of large numbers of fire fighters on Van Ness to save the Western Addition had left the area behind them almost unprotected.

By dawn the new fire front had already reached Russian Hill and was heading east toward Telegraph Hill and the North Beach area. There was to be no rest for the exhausted fire fighters. Wearily they moved their battered equipment on to begin another stubborn battle.

On Russian Hill, householders had watched the flames eat through the five blocks between them and Nob Hill. They had made a gallant effort to save their homes. Using water stored in sinks and bathtubs, they had wet down bedding, drapes, and old clothing. They had tried to beat out blazing sparks and smoldering embers as they lit, but the fury of the fire had been too much for them. By dawn the south and west slopes of the hill had burned. On the crest, however, two blocks of houses still resisted the flames.

Soldiers, arriving with the firemen, looked up to the top of the hill to see a strangely moving sight. The flag under which they served was being raised above a large shingled house. Three times the Stars and Stripes dipped, as if in final salute to enemy flames. Then its bright folds streamed out against the black fog of smoke.

The flag was a battle cry to the soldiers. They could not let its challenge go unanswered. Clambering up the hill, they broke open the door and rushed into the house. Using water found in tubs and siphon bottles, smothering flames with damp sand from a house under construction across the street, they saved the house under the brave flag.

The man who had raised the flag was a Civil War veteran who made a hobby of collecting flags. When the owner of the home had left to take his sick wife across the bay, the old soldier had stayed on in the two rooms he rented. As fire approached, he had chosen the best of his flags and defiantly run it up the flagstaff atop the house. Dipping it in salute to defeat, he had prepared to leave. The arrival of the soldiers and their gallant effort made it possible for him to stay on. When the owners returned a few days later, the old soldier was there to tell his story triumphantly.

The hilltop escaped destruction, but below, on the level ground in the dip between Russian and Telegraph hills, fire had its way. Flames were sucked down into the area as if into a huge vacuum. People left their burning homes and bolted north toward the bay, fire racing after them on three sides. Escape seemed impossible. They were in a blazing trap. There was very

real panic. Men rushed here and there, trying to find a hole
through the wall of fire. Women screamed. Thousands pushed
and shoved their way toward the bay, where only a few launches
were available for rescue work. Crammed together on the beach,
the crowd waited in terror, while behind them firemen fought the
flames and soldiers dynamited in desperation.

Once on the waterfront, the trapped people became fairly
orderly, but there were some whose only concern was for safety
at any cost. A woman, carrying her baby, started up the gangplank to a launch. A strong man forgot decency. Shoving her so
hard that she fell into the water, he took her place. At once a
soldier sprang forward and thrust the man aside with a bayonet,
while others pulled the woman and child from the water.

When General Funston learned of the firetrap on North
Beach, he sent every boat on the bay to carry away the endan-
gered people. Even one old tugboat, the *Wizard*, out of use for
years, joined the rescue fleet. Although crossing the bay in the
Wizard was almost as dangerous as facing fire, frightened
people crowded up the gangplank. Death by drowning was
preferable to burning. With the other boats, the old tug made
trip after trip across the water until all the refugees were
removed.

Afternoon came. Despite the constant dynamiting by soldiers
and the valiant efforts of firemen, the fire was spreading, turning
into one vast conflagration. To the east it was thrusting at the
foot of Telegraph Hill. On the north it was reaching toward the
waterfront. The North Beach area was gone or going. Fingers of
fire were even hurtling toward Van Ness again, threatening to
leap the avenue on its northern reaches. The Western Addition,
which firemen had battled so hard to save, was again in danger.

Out in the bay at Fort Mason, a Navy fireboat pumped water
to a long chain of fire engines and hoses strung along Van Ness
to pump water from one to the next. A fire engine failed, and the

stream of salt water stopped. Leaping forward, a quick-witted fireman thrust a hose through a manhole into the sewer and kept a flow coming until the machine could be repaired. The watching crowd cheered his action.

Fire conquered in one place merely leaped to another spot. The west side of Van Ness began to yield to the terrific heat from the east. Roofs smoldered and paint peeled. Again houses on the east side of the avenue were dynamited.

Strenuous efforts kept the fire from crossing Van Ness, but flames raged relentlessly east of the avenue, sweeping north as far as Lombard Street, only a few blocks from the bay.

On Lombard stood a house dear to San Franciscans. It was the home of the widow of Robert Louis Stevenson, the English author of *Treasure Island* and other books beloved of young people and old. The famous novelist had never lived in this house looking so much like a Scottish mansion that it might have served in one of his own tales. He had died on the island of Samoa some years before. But everyone in the city loved and respected his widow. At all costs her home must be saved.

Earlier in the day a group of writers, artists, and musicians had come to Lombard Street, determined to keep the flames from the house. When fire began to lick at the block, they were ready. None of them knew much about fighting fire, but they had the desire and the will to do what seemed impossible. There was a cistern on the hill above, drained almost dry by the fire fighters. Filling buckets, the group of artists carried what little water there was to the house, doused blankets, and smothered every blaze that started on the roof or inside. The fire rolled on. The Scottish castle still stood, blackened but whole.

By midafternoon, fire was burning in a huge semicircle from Van Ness on the west to the bay on the northeast. Fire reached the waterfront at one point and then turned south to threaten the west side of Telegraph Hill.

On Telegraph Hill lived the city's Italian residents and many Spanish Americans. Helter-skelter up the steep hillsides stood their flimsy homes, built of wood that would burn like kindling. Shanties, apartments, boarding houses were packed closely together. The hill was so steep that ladders and ropes sometimes had to be used to get from house to house—so steep also that no fire engine had enough power to make the climb.

But Telegraph Hill had men, strong men used to labor. They had sent their women and children to safety and then prepared to do battle against the flames. Their homes might be poor, but they meant to save them. Determined men lined the streets with buckets filled from cisterns. Soldiers helped by stringing a hose all the way from the bay and up the hill, but the men of Telegraph Hill were pretty much on their own. They doused blankets, sheets, burlap sacks, and clothing in water and piled them high. They stacked rakes, axes, hoes, and shovels in handy spots. They set ladders against houses to provide a quick way to roofs. Hundreds of men waited then, grim-faced, to fight the approaching fire.

Heat struck first. Below the hill to the north were warehouses and factories. They were burning now, sending up such blasting heat that for a moment men retreated before certain death. The warehouse fires swept around the base of the hill to the east. Now it was coming up the hill.

As roofs and walls began to smoke, Italians and Mexicans leaped into action. They chopped down threatened houses. With ropes they pulled down flimsy houses built on stilts and leaning into the hill. They soaked the rubble with buckets of water. Inside those houses that stood in the path of the flames, men tore down curtains, tossed out rugs, doused walls with water. They climbed ladders and pulled smoking tar paper from roofs.

Fire was coming up the hill from the north now. It was on the hill, racing through the shoddy homes jammed so close together.

The men formed bucket brigades and ax brigades. They made use of anything moist or wet. Barrels of wine were opened, their contents dumped on the flames. Even jugs of the olive oil with which Italians liked to cook served to quench small blazes.

Night came, and midnight. Still the men fought on, weary but refusing to quit. The sky was lit with a lurid red glow. Suffocating smoke swirled about the fighters. If a man fell in exhaustion, he was dragged out of the way, and another fighter took his place. The night was full of the shouts of men, the crackle of flames, and the crash of buildings as they were pulled or chopped down.

On into the dawn the heroic men labored. And then, suddenly, they began to see that they were bringing the fire on the northern slope under control. The flames slowed, began to lose strength. In front of their advance were some vacant lots that would halt the spread of fire. It could eat no farther up the hill. And over on the west slope, the fire had been held back at the foot.

Emotional Italians wept and laughed, shook hands, and embraced one another. They had won. Their hill was safe.

During their long struggle other battles were being waged below them at the harbor line. On that Friday afternoon the North Beach blaze had reached the waterfront at its northern point.

Fort Mason, with thousands of refugees crowded into its grounds, was in danger. General Funston had made ready to meet the onset of the flames. Fire engines were on hand, and a Navy fireboat was anchored offshore to pump water from the bay. Soldiers and sailors had torn down the wooden fence around the fort and leveled all the outbuildings. Soldiers waited on rooftops, ready to smother blazes. If heat or flames should explode the powder magazine—but the soldiers tried not to think of that calamity.

"FORT MASON MAY GO," Funston wired Secretary Taft that evening. "BUT WE WILL KNOW IN AN HOUR."

Fort Mason did not "go." At eleven o'clock that night Funston wired Washington: "AT THIS HOUR . . . FORT MASON IS SAFE."

The fire was now threatening the shipyards and docks that were the city's lifeline to the trade of the world. More important at the time was the fact that the piers were the means of bringing in supplies for the thousands of homeless people.

Early Friday afternoon the fire that was threatening Fort Mason reached the waterfront at the farthest pier to the north. Firemen fought heroically there and put out the blaze. But the flames, whipped by the strong northwest wind, swept on to the east around the seawall. Fire raged through factories and warehouses. A huge gas tank exploded. Lumberyards blazed. Past Telegraph Hill and on toward the Ferry Building the fire rolled.

The Ferry Building was crowded with refugees still waiting for boat passage out of the city. Relief food was piled high on the docks. In the branch post office, mail was waiting to go out. When the ferry employees received a message that the building was sure to burn, they decided to remain as long as they could. Soldiers cleared the building of refugees.

In heat so fierce that breathing was difficult, firemen and soldiers ashore and sailors in Navy tugs and fireboats fought to save the piers and the Ferry Building. Ships at the dock moved out into the bay away from the heat. Fireboats pumped streams of water on piers and warehouses. So intense was the heat that paint on the sides of the boats blistered and peeled, and sailors had to turn their hoses on the decks.

At three o'clock in the morning, the Pacific Mail dock blazed up. If the fire raged on, every pier all the way to the south would burn. The cutter *Golden Gate* immediately turned the full force of its hoses on the pier. The flames began to die down, to sputter out. On through the small hours of the morning the battle to save the docks went on.

But the fury of the fire was broken at last. At dawn the exhausted fighters knew that the last battle was won. The inferno that had held San Francisco in its relentless grip for three days and nights was over.

It was seven o'clock on Saturday morning.

11
No City, But Lots of Hope

Those San Franciscans who had slept during the troubled night awoke Saturday morning to hope. Smoke still clouded the sky. In the burned areas flames flared up here and there, but their strength was gone. Everywhere spread the rumor that the fires were under control at last.

But what of San Francisco, the beloved city, beautiful and gay? Gone was its entire business district, with its proud skyscrapers. Gone were hotels, libraries, churches, theaters, schools, museums, art galleries, banks, and hospitals. The City Hall was gutted, all its records burned. Destroyed was the transportation system—all the miles of streetcar and cable lines that had carried people up and down the steep hills. There were no utilities. Telephone and electric wires were melted down. No water came from taps.

In the burned residential areas 250,000 homes had gone up in flame. Nothing remained but smoldering rubble, scorched gardens, and skeleton trees, their leafless branches black against a smoky sky.

Many businessmen had been ruined. Drugstores, great markets, big department stores had burned to the ground with their vast stocks of goods. Men who had known wealth now faced poverty.

San Francisco was a broken city, its people confronted with problems that seemed impossible to solve. But it now had a chance to survive. A sign that showed the unconquerable spirit of its people appeared on a ruined building on Market Street:

> The cow is in the hammock
> The cat is in the lake
> The baby in the garbage can
> What difference does it make?
> There is no water and still less soap
> We have no city, but lots of hope.

Rain fell on Saturday night, pouring from leaden skies to quench the last stubborn flames and turn the thick layer of ashes into black mud. Wind whispered through empty windows in blackened walls and whistled about the skeleton towers of skyscrapers. In the hundreds of camps, rain put out the cooking fires and soaked mattresses and bedding. But the rain was welcome, for it meant the certain end of all danger from fire.

The air was clear on Sunday morning, the black clouds of smoke gone, although wisps of steam and smoke still rose from smoldering debris. The weather had turned cold. Women and children shivered beside campfires of wet wood that burned reluctantly. Men searched for dry wood. They tried to build better shelters for their families. Under such miserable conditions, the people in the camps found it hard to be cheerful, but their spirits were raised by a proclamation from Mayor Schmitz stating officially that the fire was over.

San Franciscans went to church that Sunday morning, whether there was a church of their faith to hold services in or not.

79

Mass was said on the steps of burned cathedrals or in their ruins. Thousands crowded the chapel and grounds at the Presidio. Out in Golden Gate Park, thousands more gathered before a pulpit of boxes and boards. While a man played a cornet, they sang:

Other refuge have I none, hangs my helpless soul on Thee: Leave, oh, leave me not alone: still support and comfort me.

Even in those first trying days after the fire, the people of San Francisco refused to be downed by calamity. In the parks and squares, in the little camps that sprang up wherever there was a pond or spring to provide some water, cheerful spirits were apparent in the amusing signs nailed above shelters and sidewalk kitchens.

One woman who was fortunate enough to have a tent wrote above it: RING THE BELL FOR THE LANDLADY—FURNISHED ROOMS WITH RUNNING WATER, STEAM HEAT AND ELEVATOR. Another crude shelter displayed the sign: COME IN AND SPEND A QUIET EVENING.

Mayor Schmitz's proclamation had ordered those whose homes had not burned to refrain from building fires in stoves until all chimneys could be inspected. As a result, all cooking was done in the street. Some homeowners built barbecues of brick with a metal sheet over the top to hold pots and pans; others moved small stoves or kitchen ranges out into the open.

In the camps women shared community kitchens. Many funny signs appeared:

CHEER UP. HAVE ONE ON ME.

THE PALACE GRILL.

THE FAIRMONT—THE UNFAIRMONT.

BON-TON BEANERY.

SKIDOO CAFE—WANTED, A BOY TO BRUSH FLIES
    OFF GUESTS.

Even business-as-usual signs began to appear, such as DON'T TALK FIRE: TALK BUSINESS. One man displayed this placard above his thrown-together shack:

> FIRST TO SHAKE
> FIRST TO BURN
> FIRST TO TAKE
> ANOTHER NEW TURN.

Cheer, forced or real, was the order of the day among the homeless. Living was not easy, but it helped to make the best of things. For parents and the elderly, camp life was hard, but to the children it was one long outdoor picnic. There were no schools to confine them. It was fun to eat their meals in the sun and sleep under the stars. Since there was little water, no one could urge them to wash or change into clean clothing. And always there were plenty of playmates for games.

Mayor Schmitz, the Committee for Safety, the Army, and the police force had new problems to face at the beginning of the week. Streets in the burned areas were clogged with piles of rubble that had to be moved away before pavings could be mended. Tangled streetcar rails had to be repaired and cable and telephone wires replaced. Broken water mains and gas lines had to be mended. In the crowded camps there was great danger of epidemics unless sanitation rules were enforced. The mayor at once issued orders for the digging of garbage pits and sanitary trenches.

By far the biggest and most pressing problem was the feeding of more than 300,000 homeless people. At first there was great confusion in the distribution of the carloads of provisions and medical supplies that were pouring into the city from Oakland, the terminus of the transcontinental railway. Mayor Schmitz and the committee undertook the task, with the aid of the soldiers.

Ruins of City Hall

On Monday, however, a Red Cross official, Dr. Edward T. Devine, arrived in San Francisco. He had been sent by President Roosevelt to take charge of all relief work and of the funds that were coming in from all over the world. San Franciscans were angry. They could take care of themselves, they said. Mayor Schmitz might have been guilty of graft in the past, but he had proved himself a leader in the days of crisis. Why not let the mayor and his committee handle the relief work?

However, Dr. Devine, who had years of experience in such work, proved so tactful and efficient that anger was soon forgotten. Under his direction the Red Cross eventually took over all relief work. The Army was assigned the task of protecting health and policing property.

Famine had been the great fear at first. By Monday there was no reason for that fear. By ship and train, loads of food arrived and kept on coming. From cities, large and small, across the nation rolled boxcars bearing signs reading, FOR THE CALIFORNIA SUFFERERS.

Housewives of Ogden, Utah, served no bread to their families for days. All loaves were sent to San Francisco. Boys of an Indian school in Oregon pooled their savings and baked 830 loaves to send to the sufferers. In many towns all over the United States, children were excused from school to collect food.

Instead of famine, San Francisco soon found itself embarrassed by a wealth of the kind of food not easily usable. Homeless women had no pans for cooking potatoes, no ovens to bake flour into bread. Although fresh meat was needed, there was no way of butchering or pasturing the hundreds of head of cattle that were driven in. Finally, butchers set up boards and boxes in the streets and cut and distributed beef. Canned goods, however, remained scarce, and men still combed the debris for blackened tins of food.

Centers for distributing provisions were soon set up—more

than 175 of them. The long lines in front of them were an example of democracy. No person was favored. Rich and poor stood for hours in line as they waited for an equal dole. Food could not be bought. If you were hungry, you stood in line. A few people may have grumbled, but most of them accepted the hardship cheerfully. They were rather proud of the fact that all were equal, and odd friendships were formed.

Charles K. Field wrote of the good humor of San Franciscans in those days. In his poem he had a poor Irish woman tell her experiences in the bread line:

> An' Mrs. Van Bergen she greets me these days
> With a smile an' a nod of her head;
> "Ah, Mrs. McGinnis, how are you?" she says,
> "An' do you like government bread?"
> She fetches a bag made of crockydile skin
> An' I've got a sack when we meet,
> But the same kind of coffee and crackers goes in,
> An' it's all of it cooked in the street.
> Sure Mrs. Van Bergen is takin' it fine,
> Ye'd think she was used to such food;
> We're gettin' acquainted a-standin' in line,
> An' it's doin' the both of us good.

Later, hot food stations were set up in the streets, and millions of meals were served on long tables, with rough benches for seats. If a hungry person had fifteen cents, he paid it for a dinner of soup, roast beef or hash, hot biscuits, and coffee. If he had no money, the Red Cross gave him a free ticket, and he ate the same food.

Food was not the only aid that poured into San Francisco in the days after the fire. In addition to the total relief fund voted by Congress—$2,500,000—more money came in from this nation and the world. Of foreign nations, Japan contributed the most;

the total from all of them amounted to nearly $475,000. More and more money came—from Los Angeles, New York City, Philadelphia, the state of Massachusetts. The Salvation Army, the Red Cross, and various other organizations collected money on the streets of many cities in the United States.

Entertainers performed and sent the money to San Francisco. The Barnum and Bailey Circus donated a day's take at the ticket window. The great actress Sarah Bernhardt gave benefit performances. So did actress Marie Dressler. George M. Cohan, of song-and-dance fame, sold papers on the streets of New York. One paper alone brought $1,000. Jim Jeffries, heavyweight boxing champion, peddled oranges in Los Angeles for $20 a dozen. Many other famous performers gave street shows to raise money.

With the aid of these generous donations and through the courage and determination of its people, San Francisco would be built again.

12
To Build Anew

The tremendous task of mopping up the devastation left by earthquake and fire had begun even before the flames had subsided. Down Market Street, a path had been cleared through which a slender stream of traffic could move. As soon as the fire was over, hired laborers and volunteers began moving the debris from clogged streets and buildings.

In the cellars of the burned St. Francis Hotel, they found Francis, a small white dog. Through four days and nights he had survived without food. Francis became one of the heroes of the fire, and his picture was printed on postcards and sold everywhere.

Temporary rails were built that could carry flatcars loaded with debris to the bay, where it was dumped into the water. Trucks and wagons aided in the labor.

Beneath the rubble the streets proved to be not too much damaged. Many sewers and underground water lines were still intact, and plumbers began work at once to repair the broken ones. To restore water to San Francisco was a matter of repairing the mains that led from reservoirs outside the city. The work already in progress there was completed, and in ten days water flowed from taps in many unburned homes.

One of the most necessary projects was to put the destroyed banks into operation again. Bankers who had carted money away from the fire brought it back and set up business wherever they could find space. Some built temporary structures over undamaged vaults; others turned homes into banks. Money was soon circulating again.

Downtown San Francisco looked for a time as it had in the boom days of the gold rush of 1849. On Market Street, crude, unpainted shacks mushroomed on the site of old business buildings. Flimsy wooden restaurants and sidewalk cafés sold simple and cheap meals. Peddlars sold souvenirs, junk, and pictures of the fire. Smiths hammered at street forges to keep shoes on the thousands of horses used for hauling away debris. Sign painters and men who could open the many damaged safes set up shops in the open. The streets were crowded with people. Unlike the early miners, however, they drank lemonade, bought from a street stand. The sale of liquor was forbidden for a time, and no saloons were open to encourage fights or shooting frays. Anyway, people were much too busy for the foolish gunplay of the gold rush days.

There was work for everybody. Dangerous buildings were dynamited, and the removal of rubble was completed. Electric, wire, and telephone services were restored. A few streetcars ran again. The city newspapers were published from Oakland while new offices were built. Some of the relief funds were used to encourage small businesses to start again — grocery stores, laundries, meat markets, boardinghouses. Also, many small grants were made to laborers so that they could buy new tools for their trades.

Building went on everywhere, some temporary, some permanent. The Emporium, the largest department store in the West,

Ruins near the Ferry Building

opened in quarters built onto its undamaged front and later put up a new building on Van Ness. Out on Nob Hill, the Fairmont's new marble walls still stood, blackened by fire, but work was begun to restore the gutted interior. Other hotels started construction. New banks were built. The mansions saved from fire on the west side of Van Ness were converted into offices and shops. All along Van Ness, flags flew in the sea breeze to prove the undaunted spirit of San Franciscans.

And what of the homeless? The tents provided by the Army arrived a few days after the fire, and tent cities grew up where some of the larger camps had been. The city also built thousands of wooden huts, crowded together so closely that there was scarcely walking room between them. Life was not pleasant in the hut camps, but people were thankful to have roofs and walls to keep out fog and rain. Besides, the occupants later were allowed to move their huts to their own lots, where burned homes had stood. Many a hut became the beginning of a larger house.

Many San Franciscans thought that Chinatown, with its evil opium and gambling dens, should not be rebuilt. If the Chinese want a place of their own, people said, let them move to the outskirts of town. The Chinese were polite, but stubborn. They owned the land in Chinatown, and there they would stay. As one Chinese put it, "By and by, we build all new." That is what they did, putting up better structures, this time more picturesquely Chinese in architecture. Chinatown bloomed again with bright color and quaint shops.

"By and by, we build all new" is what all the people of San Francisco resolved to do. In three years the almost unbelievable task had been accomplished, the burned areas restored. Although the great fire had given the city a chance to beautify itself, there was no time for planning. Some of the streets were widened, a new city center was built around the restored City

Hall, and taller skyscrapers dwarfed those of the days before the fire. But the new San Francisco was much like the old city.

In 1915, San Francisco proudly invited the world to come to the Panama-Pacific International Exposition, held there to celebrate the opening of the Panama Canal. To visitors the celebration was a salute to the courageous spirit that had created a new city from the ashes of the old.

Bibliography

BRONSON, WILLIAM, *The Earth Shook, the Sky Burned*. New York, Doubleday & Company, Inc., 1959.

DOLAN, EDWARD F., JR., *Disaster 1906*. New York, Julian Messner, Inc., 1967.

IACOPI, ROBERT, *Earthquake Country*. Menlo Park, California, Lane Books, 1965.

JACKSON, CHARLOTTE, *The Story of San Francisco*. New York, Random House, 1955.

KENNEDY, JOHN CASTILLO, *The Great Earthquake and Fire*. New York, William Morrow and Company, 1963.

KOCH, WALTER, *San Francisco: The Illustrated History*. San Francisco, The Ken Books, 1966.

SUTHERLAND, MONICA, *The Damnedest Finest Ruins*. New York, Coward-McCann, Inc., 1959.

Index

93

INDEX

The Colorful and Exciting

SAGAS OF THE WEST
From G. P. Putnam's Sons

FIRST WAGONS TO CALIFORNIA
by Michael Chester   Illustrated by Steele Savage

COLONEL ANZA'S IMPOSSIBLE JOURNEY
by Jonreed Lauritzen   Illustrated by Steele Savage

FLAG OF THE DREADFUL BEAR
by Robert West Howard   Illustrated by Albert Orbaan

FORTS OF OLD CALIFORNIA
by Michael Chester   Illustrated by Steele Savage

THE BATTLE OF SAN PASQUAL
by Jonreed Lauritzen   Illustrated by Leon Gregori

JOSEPH STRAUSS:
BUILDER OF THE GOLDEN GATE BRIDGE
by Michael Chester   Illustrated by Tom Hamil

THE ADVENTURES OF GRIZZLY ADAMS
by Jean Muir   Illustrated by Albert Orbaan

THE SAN FRANCISCO EARTHQUAKE AND FIRE
by Helen Markley Miller   Illustrated by Albert Orbaan

The Author

HELEN MARKLEY MILLER received her B.A. from the State College of Iowa and her M.A. from Western State College, Colorado. Besides writing nearly a score of books, she has taught school, written for newspapers, and traveled widely throughout the United States by car and trailer. Mrs. Miller now lives in McCall, Idaho.